THIS JOURNAL BELONGS TO

_____

INTRODUCTION

Mother Mary has watched over me my entire life. Her signature grace seems to arise when I don't realise that I need it. Time and time again before unexpected and potentially difficult happenings in my life, she has appeared in some form. However, I never feel afraid or feel a sense of doom. I simply feel her loving presence and am grateful to connect with her.

As one of her sacred symbols, ladybugs have shown up in my life many times when I needed to know that everything was going to be okay. They are not her only sign, of course. Sometimes I see her in a vision in meditation or sense her in my heart. An unexpected gift of roses is another of her hallmarks in my life.

Your connection with Mother Mary might happen in other ways. She loves all of us equally and will connect with us in whatever ways are best. That is one reason I have written projects dedicated to her — because I know that for many people, they are a wonderful avenue for her to reach their hearts.

Many years ago, I accidentally bumped my foot against a hard bamboo bath mat. It hurt a lot more than I thought was possible, and I wondered if I had broken my toe! Having never had a broken bone, I was extremely nervous at the prospect of it. I instantly began thinking about not being able to do my beloved yoga practice for weeks on end, and I talked myself into quite a state of anxiety! I booked in to see my doctor immediately.

In my enthusiasm to get to the appointment — hoping to have my mind soothed — I arrived too early. I sat outside in the sunshine and waited for the time when I would need to brave the doctor's office. Then I felt something ever so lightly moving on my arm. I glanced down to see a tiny ladybug travelling carefully along my forearm. I knew it was a sign from Mother Mary that everything was going to be okay.

I was surprised then when my doctor said my toe was probably broken and to stay off it for many weeks. She sent me to get an x-ray. I was puzzled but kept thinking of that little ladybug. The x-ray technician said I would have to wait at least a day for the doctor to interpret the results, but for some reason, she decided to tell me the outcome then and there — no break. It was a sprain. I prayed for healing, and within a few days, I was back in my yoga class.

Those little ladybugs have granted me signs of hope in Australia, in Tibet, and even in Utah where I was travelling for a book tour. In Utah, I had a late evening flight that I couldn't change and the checkout time for the Airbnb I was staying at was 10am. My flight was nearly twelve hours later. I had massive suitcases, as I had been travelling for months. I would have loved to spend the day wandering about exploring Salt Lake City instead of in a tiny airport. I thought a late evening checkout was pushing it, but I asked. Several days passed without any answer, and I was getting concerned. I thought about booking a day room in a hotel somewhere. When I tried to log on to the day room websites, my computer froze. That happened twice. I felt it was a sign.

Later that afternoon, at my yoga class, I noticed an adorable little ladybug had found her way onto my yoga mat! I gently lifted her from the mat and placed her on a blade of grass. I knew that Mother Mary was letting me know she was taking care of things. After my class, I received a message from the Airbnb host saying that no-one was checking in the next day and she'd didn't mind me having a late checkout. In fact, she was happy for me to stay as long as I wished at no additional cost.

Mary has guided me through the challenges that have felt the most demanding, from the sudden need to find a new place to live to the times when I needed to walk away from a person I loved because the relationship wasn't healthy for me. She was there from the anxiety-inducing possibilities that turned out to be nothing to worry about to the revelations that required courage to process while finding grace, dignity, and gratitude. I experience her as an active, kind, powerful, and protective presence in my life. I know she is a Divine Mother to all souls who will open their hearts to her.

It is to her all-loving and unfailingly true heart that I offer this work. May all hearts in need of her be open to receive her blessing, guidance, and grace.

Alana Fairchild

Do you believe I could forget or deny you?
You have belonged to me through all time and are my divine child.
You are under my care and protection.
Let go of your worries now and pray to me.
I will assist you.

You have outgrown what has been, and the manifestation of the new is only a matter of time. Growth must happen now. Trust your unfolding path.

Remember, you are not only being guided away from what has been
but toward a new dawn.

Visualise yourself surrounded by a beautiful field of blue light.
Allow yourself to feel truly safe and held, as though that light is a soft divine
blanket of comfort and protection for your mind, body, and soul.

I want to be close to you, my cherished child, so I dwell within your heart.

The clearest guidance is not always the loudest. Sometimes fear and doubt yell, while love and trust speak quietly but consistently from deep within the heart. It is wise to trust in the truths of your heart, even when they seem quieter than the voices of fear arising within or coming from those around you.

Hearing the truth of the heart may necessitate action that you would rather not take. However, Our Lady speaks to you of courage, trust, and her loving protection as you honour your heart.

What miracle is calling you by name? What story have you been telling yourself about why there isn't more peace. What is it you want? What opening in the clouds are you seeking? Ask and then find your yes amongst all the previous no thank yous. Today is a good day for miracles

To find the
Way through...
Enter the Heart

Shiloh 2008

Silent Sound Healing

There are spiritual sounds that only the soul can hear. These spiritual sounds are unnoticeable, silent from a physical perspective, but they resonate deeply at a subtle yet powerful inner level. These sounds have positive effects within the spiritual heart, creating pathways for healing the mind, body, and soul.

The divine beings of light, such as our beloved Mother Mary, understand how to create these sacred sounds in a willing heart. They know the precise vibration that is needed to create the best healing outcomes for you on all levels.

May our hearts and minds be open to such wisdom and healing grace. May all beings in need, receive.

A SILENT SOUND HEALING

You can conduct this exercise for yourself by reading it aloud or recording it on a mobile device and playing it back for yourself. If you wish to offer it for others, you can read it aloud. Remember to leave time and space for visualisation after each instruction. If you or another cannot visualise well, that is fine. Instead of trying to visualise or imagine something, allow yourself to feel. Notice any emotions, feelings, or sensations in response to the descriptions. You might feel peace, relaxation, or a release of emotion. Just be with your experience and know that it is valuable.

We work with the colour white in this exercise, as white light holds all the colours (and therefore all the frequencies or vibrations) within it. From that white light, the best rainbow medicine will be distilled for your particular needs at this time.

Find a place to relax and focus, a place where you are unlikely to be disturbed. Turn any devices to silent mode if possible.

See, sense, or feel the presence of a large, white bell created from pure light.

A radiant woman of light wears a white robe and a crown of white roses. She steps forward and strikes the bell with one clear and purposeful movement.

Pure, powerful resonance rings out. It is a sound of silence that is felt in every fibre of your soul. The sacred sound of silence echoes deeply through all dimensions and layers of your being.

Intend to receive that sound for a few moments, and know it is helping to support you as you elevate your frequency. You don't have to understand how it happens; it just happens.

Rest in this space for as long as you feel is right for you.

The woman in white gazes directly at you. You can hide nothing from her, and you realise she sees you through the divine eye of love and supports you unconditionally. You don't need to hide. You are seen, loved, and recognised. You may feel some release from the heart and self-forgiveness arising.

Rest in this silent communication of deep love and spaciousness for as long as feels best.

When you are ready to close your healing process, you can say the following affirmative prayer:

Mother Mary, I receive your sacred sound of silence. It cleanses me on all levels and creates wisdom, love, and compassion. May the healing sounds reverberate deep in the souls of all beings in need. I open myself to your healing now, on every level of my being, so I may release the past, be open to the present moment, and honour my sacred life path for the greatest good of all. May all hearts know your healing presence.

Take some time to ground yourself and hydrate your body. You have completed your sacred practice.

You have her guiding light within to support you through the changes in your life.
Even unwanted change will be something you are soon grateful to have embraced.

Sometimes sadness is a necessary offering at the threshold of greater
happiness and sacred fulfilment.

You shall thrive and be nourished into life. Your uniqueness and beauty shall not be obscured by fear and shame. Hers is the holy hand unveiling your secret light so it may pour forth, increasing love in our world.

Pray with courage and conviction. Cultivate a sense of inevitability
rather than hopeful fantasy. Now is not the time to hold back and
compromise on what is possible. Instead, surrender the 'how' to the
Divine Mother and allow her to guide you into sacred fulfilment.

No one can replicate the unique expression of the Divine that you are.
No one can live your destiny for you. You have a distinct role and purpose
upon this Earth. Each being is destined to become their true nature as fully
and completely as the heart can dare.

You may be uncertain of your future, about what is happening within you, or even whether anything is happening at all. Take steps that feel loving, one at a time, one after the other, trusting and knowing that they are the loving prompts of the Divine Mother as she nurtures you into the fullness of being.

Becoming requires energy. We do not have to throw ourselves mercilessly into endless activity or be anxious that we must do something, even while not knowing what we are supposed to be doing! Trust yourself. Trust the Divine Mother. Replenish yourself and have faith in your process and your timing.

Speak this from your heart: "My becoming is assured. I am a unique divine blossom in the Holy Mother's garden of life. I am nurtured, nourished, and supported as I now become all that I am through the protective care of her grace-filled hands. I am. I am. I am."

Honour the light that is ignited within you now, and act upon it with utter faith.

Feel for her voice in your heart saying:
"All will come to you, my beloved. Nothing shall be withheld."

Trust in the generosity of the divine harvest, the fruits of your labours,
and the blessings of grace that fill your life.

To grow and blossom, the soul needs honesty more than it needs pleasantness. We need the light of joy and also the darkness of anger, grief, and sadness to vitalise and cleanse us. When we accept our life experiences and grow through them, we are actively manifesting our divine destiny.

Becoming a divinely awakened human being is a raw, wild, and beautiful path that often involves great suffering. Our Madonna feels great compassion for, and understanding of, what it is to be human. So, she empowers us, through her wisdom, to take the journey with fearless faith in her divine protection and guidance.

ning For The Divine Instruction.

Shiloh

Mourning Loss and Welcoming Renewal

It is a paradox that when we are open to life, we can feel like parts of ourselves and our lives die numerous symbolic deaths. We might experience the ending of relationships, ideals, identities, even certain hopes and dreams, with such intensity and significance that we feel as though we have gone through a powerful symbolic death, and our lives can never be the same again.

At other times, it will be the physical passing of a loved one, perhaps even a soul animal companion, or a dearly beloved partner, child, or friend that breaks our heart in grief. Mother Mary witnessed the death of her beloved son. She is no stranger to grief, loss, and the agony that these experiences can evoke in the human heart. She knows how we suffer, and she knows how we can find the courage to heal.

If we can mourn these deaths, give them proper attention and due acknowledgement, grieving in whatever way is respectful and truthful, then those deaths become sacred sacrifices on the altar of new life. We can grow through the loss, becoming wiser and more compassionate humans, capable of holding space for others to also become brave enough to experience their losses and mature spiritually through the process.

If we try to rush past these experiences, pushing them to one side out of fear that they may mean something terrible or frightening, or that we do not have the strength to bear the loss, then we will suffer more, not less. We may become fearful if we feel we are not in control of life and cannot prevent its powerful unfolding because we do not trust where it is leading us. Then, too, we miss our chance to make a sacrifice and feel more connected with life and with death as a natural part of our journey.

We don't have to be scared of such losses, as painful as they may be. We can accept that they are signs that life is unfolding. In response, we can become more grateful for the time we have with this precious body and this unique life. As painful as it can be, we can choose to continue our journey, knowing that an ending always signals a beginning. We may then realise that we don't need to be afraid and that we have all we need within our hearts to flourish.

YOUR SACRED PRACTICE

Find a place where you will not be disturbed and can relax. If you wish to have tokens of the past that signify what you are releasing (photographs or a piece of clothing, for example), place those nearby. If you wish to have symbols that evoke the promise of a new life for you (such as aspirational images or a beautiful flower or a crystal), you can have those near you, too. You do not need such objects to complete the ritual, but they can be powerful if you feel inclined to include them.

Place your attention on your left hand. Lightly touch any symbolic objects that relate to the past or keep your left hand open, ready to receive.

Sense the connection between your left hand and the energy lines that flow to and from your heart. Within your heart is a radiant white light, and within that light is the blessed Madonna, shining her love and healing.

Allow her blessing of light to flow from your heart to your hand. When you are ready, hold the intention to offer the past to Mary.

Can you honour your pain? Can you find any gratitude for something you learned or received from the past? Claim that for yourself while leaving all else behind.

You may like to express a simple prayer now, such as:

Beloved Mother Mary, I offer this to you entirely. Please bless and heal all aspects of this experience. May it become sacred learning for all involved. May your grace and love transform suffering into wisdom and compassion. I open myself completely to your healing love and take shelter in your spiritual protection.

Take your time and sense Mary pouring white light through every part of the experience, your own heart, and any connection that remains between you and the past. This is her purification, blessing, and protection. Let your heart settle. Let it be.

See, sense, or feel how the past has brought you to where you are now. You have nothing to regret and nothing to fear. You are ready to ground yourself in the present moment. In Mary's presence, you are able to take one step after another, making authentic choices with respect for yourself and the value of your journey.

Take your time and put any objects representing the past to one side. They can be placed into storage later with peace in your heart.

Now turn your attention to the right hand. Touch any sacred objects that relate to your positive view of the future or keep your right hand open to Mother Mary. Sense the connection between your right hand and your heart. Sense the presence of the beloved Madonna in your heart as a golden pink light.

Allow her golden pink light to flow from your heart to your right hand, infusing your sacred objects and/or your entire being with her beautiful golden pink light.

Let yourself be filled with this healing, strengthening energy. Breathe, relax, and imagine or intend to receive it. If you can, allow it to feel good.

When you are ready, you may like to express a simple prayer, such as:

Beloved Mother Mary, I trust in your guardianship and guidance for my unfolding life path. Please bless me and help me recognise that I have the courage and wisdom to walk this path with dignity and grace. May your strength of spirit touch and heal all hearts. May all beings find true fulfilment.

Take your time now to relax. Rest with Mother Mary in this space of dignity and unconditional regard for as long as you wish. You may like to imagine sending those loving qualities from your heart to all beings in need.

You have completed your sacred practice. If you have included any objects representing the past in this practice, mindfully place them in storage with peace in your heart.

When we understand there is potential for healing in all experiences, that we draw to us what we need when we need it, and that the Divine Mother protects us whenever we call upon her, we can trust. We might not always understand, but we can still choose to trust. Through our trust, we gain access to growth, healing, and miraculous grace.

When the soul is allowed to live, rather than made to fit within the confines of the logical mind, miracles can occur.

As the heart opens to life without restraint, the miraculous love of the Mother
can flow through us. We become instruments of her grace.

Affirm: "Golden Mother, burning bright with heavenly love, you honour the needs of my soul. Wild and free, it must be fed by darkness and light. Watch over and bless me with all I need to become my most radiant aliveness. Through the holy miracles of your grace, I remember you and I are always one, and the world is nourished by our love."

I have many names and faces, but behind those names and faces, I am your loving mother, always. I come to you in light and darkness, through joy and even, my beloved, through loss and tragedy. I am seeking you, reaching for you, calling you to me. If you can know this, then great peace and spiritual power will be yours, and together we shall infuse this world with love.

The dark face of Mother Mary manifests as the powerful Black Madonna, who initiates us through the challenges of human experience and bears our suffering along with us. Through her powerful presence, we learn that a pure heart can always manifest love, even in suffering.

You are called to this path at this particular time in your life
because it will serve you most and you are ready.

Lady Grace
by
Shiloh Sophia

She calls to you through the experiences of suffering that will break your heart open into a greater capacity for bliss and rapture. She acknowledges all that you bear on your path for the greater purpose of awakening. Her love sanctifies every aspect of your suffering, so that it may ultimately lead you to love. All that you give will be returned to you and multiplied as grace and miracles. Do not turn away.

*Her spiritual power and grace flow through those of us with hearts strong
enough to bear honest experiences of painful but liberating emotions, such
as sadness and grief, anger and rage (including divine outrage), and allow
these feelings to stretch our hearts' ability to love.*

You are helping to release the pain of the world.

She reassures us that we will move through this time of struggle.
She is with us always.

Through our ability to be fearlessly open to life, we are asked to bear suffering and are blessed with a capacity for divine rapture. Trust in the heart opening that is taking place for you. From pain, there will be light.

Now is your time. Pray for help to trust her wisdom and receive her blessings with a courageous heart. Your life will be transformed through her grace.

Lady Hope
Hears our
Heart

the
Love
of the Mama
heals
all

Asking for Spiritual Assistance

One of the simplest and most potent spiritual techniques available to increase the ease and grace in our lives is to ask for divine help each day from the guidance that loves us unconditionally. You may have a clear sense of who your guides are, but more likely than not, you are not so sure.

Fortunately, your guidance knows you and loves you, and you can recognise them by the feelings of love, peace, and comfort that they evoke in your heart, even if you don't have a name or a face to allocate to those guides. I don't have names or faces to associate with many of my spiritual team. Yet I know them by feeling so well! Learning to trust feelings beyond appearances leads to higher quality intuition and discernment, so there is a benefit to not knowing the names or faces of your guides and trusting in your heart connection nonetheless.

Every human has a loving spiritual team helping them fulfil their life path and purpose. When you succeed spiritually, every being on Earth benefits. Higher spiritual guidance operates on a win-win basis. Whatever you ask your higher guidance for assistance with will benefit the entire human race. So, you can let go of any lower frequency ideas that it is selfish to ask for help or that you should be a lone wolf and do everything on your own. Such ideas might seem noble, but they are foolish, undermine your progress, and make it harder for your guidance to help you. They also make it harder for you to benefit all those many beings who would be uplifted by your growing spiritual presence and light.

As Mother Mary has the spiritual goal of liberating all living beings, she very much wants you to connect, not only with her but with your entire team of spiritual guides. It matters not whether those guides are tribal elders from other lifetimes, star beings that resonate with unconditional love, angels, ascended masters, or a combination of some or all of these and more. What matters is that you get into the divinely helpful habit of making daily heartfelt requests for assistance in all ways, for the highest good.

We live in a universe of free will, and although there are legions of angels and other spiritual guides awaiting our call, they are not empowered to act on our behalf until we ask. So, let us use our free will with wisdom and call on the pure, enlightened, loving spiritual guides that are genuinely helpful and spiritually empowered to do good for all beings and to alleviate suffering and help us all find freedom, peace, happiness, and love.

YOUR SACRED PRACTICE

This practice is sacred and simple. Find a place where you can be undisturbed for a few moments. Connect with your heart. You can do this simply by placing a hand on your heart. Then say the following prayer, or your preferred variation, quietly in your mind or, when possible, aloud.

> *I call on Mother Mary and the enlightened spiritual guidance that loves me unconditionally. I ask for your protection, intervention, and assistance in all ways that bring spiritual benefit to all beings. Thank you.*

Take a moment to feel love and gratitude in your heart.

You have completed your sacred practice.

If you wish, you can say this prayer every morning before rising and every evening before retiring. Every time you say the prayer, you strengthen your connection to your spiritual team, and their presence will feel increasingly conscious and tangible for you.

There are no limits to her capacity when you are truly devoted to her.
Pray to her with complete confidence and trust.

*Prayer is speaking with the Divine from the heart. There is no
need for ornate words or perfect expression. Whatever comes
from your heart is the most powerful prayer.*

"Mother Mary, be with me, guide me, protect me, and assist me, so that I can serve love. Thank you." *Say this and be dressed in an invisible yet palpable robe of protection and grace.*

Be strong but do not 'toughen up.' A soft, receptive heart —
rather than a heart hardened by fear or the expectation of disappointment —
can be touched by the Divine more easily.

Your prayer can be resolved. Your prayer will be answered.
Let go of your fear. Hold on to your faith.

A prayer for faith: "Mother Mary, help me find the courage to accept the answers to all my prayers. Help me surrender my thoughts on how this should be and lovingly embrace what is. I trust you completely. I thank you for your divine intervention and protection. May I feel that you are with me, always. The heartfelt prayers of the world are answered through your miraculous grace."

Whatever you release shall become sacred fertiliser for your new life.
I promise that as you trust in me, I will guide you to the fulfilment of
your heart's destiny. Do not shy away from what I ask of you.

Nuestra
Señora
Maestosa

_____

_____

_____

_____

_____

_____

_____

_____

_____

_____

_____

_____

_____

_____

_____

_____

_____

_____

_____

_____

_____

_____

_____

_____

_____

She promises us that our trust in her will never be misplaced. At times when your life is pushing you beyond your limits and you feel that you are breaking, your trust in her must become stronger. It will help you receive her soothing presence, like the glow from a lighthouse that illuminates the way for safe passage through the darkest night.

No matter what appears to be, soul birth is happening for you now, and all that is manifesting is a symptom of that. Have faith in the fundamental goodness of everything occurring within you. Trust that she is looking out for you. Believe in the kindness of your destiny.

Pray: "Holy Mother Mary, who loves me unconditionally, I surrender into the process of transformation. I offer my suffering on the altar of new life. May my inner eye see you so that no matter what appears to be on the surface, I know that I need not fear, for a blessing of new life is awakening within me now."

_____

_____

_____

_____

_____

_____

_____

_____

_____

_____

_____

_____

_____

_____

_____

_____

_____

_____

_____

Declare: "I am letting go of the past, and the past is letting go of me. I am free to love and be loved, to be all that I can be. Holy Mother Mary promises me new life and is guiding me to the fulfilment of my heart's destiny."

Your purpose is your way of being, living, and giving on this planet.
You are here in your precious body to fulfil your destiny in service to the
great divine plan of love. You have the Divine on your side!
Is there any greater support and assurance of success?

Our Lady of Lourdes brings Living Water

Presence of peace

Love's Alchemy for Karmic Clearing

Karma is not bad luck nor punishment; it is simply spiritual homework that helps your soul learn. Some homework is enjoyable, and some will likely have you pulling your hair out, wanting to skip school for the rest of your life and escape to a tropical island (perhaps with internet access, air-conditioning, and an organic farmer's market specialising in gluten-free deliciousness). Yet dealing with our challenges — our karma — with the viewpoint that we aren't being punished but empowered to grow is ultimately more helpful in manifesting our dreams.

When you are suffering, it can be hard to fathom that any good can come of it. Yet you have already had difficult times in your life that helped you become a stronger, wiser, freer and more compassionate person. If you can relate to that, then you've been able to transform your karma into spiritual growth. You've been a spiritual alchemist.

Love is the magic ingredient in spiritual alchemy. It keeps us strong enough and brave enough to keep going with some seed of trust in our hearts, even when we cannot know how it is all going to be right again in our lives. If we can access a deep spiritual love, it can take the edge off the pain and provide us with enough challenge for our growth but not so much that we feel absolutely overcome and broken into a billion tiny pieces.

Old souls often have big challenges. Like an advanced student given more advanced homework, these challenges can help them develop their great potential. Old souls face those trials because they have the spiritual capacity to endure and transform. Greater challenge can bring greater benefit.

Younger souls will not yet have the courage and the strength to go through such a thing. However, recognising that you are an old soul doesn't mean your life has to become increasingly difficult as you grow spiritually. It is possible to experience deeper challenges with less suffering when you are in divine connection with the Holy Mother. You will feel pain, yes, but also the loving wisdom that helps guide you into healing and freedom.

Mother Mary knows this and wants to help all souls — young and old — to attain their spiritual fulfilment, to grow and express their beautiful soul light, and to overcome old patterns that would prevent this.

This is a significant karmic time for you. It heralds the assistance of the Divine Mother in working through challenging karma and the blessing of the Divine Mother bestowed through supportive and uplifting karmic inheritance. There is a time, you see, not only to learn but also to earn the reward of past efforts. We might call the blessings that follow the hard-won breakthroughs in our lives positive karma or a sacred harvest.

The following sacred practice will help you attract divine assistance to meet challenges and the openness to harvest your spiritual rewards. These are both being offered to you now in acknowledgement of your past efforts and all the good that your spiritual success can bring to the world around you.

THE KARMIC ALCHEMY HEALING PRACTICE

You can conduct this exercise by reading it aloud or recording it on a mobile device and playing it back for yourself. If you wish to offer it for others, you can read it aloud. Remember to leave time and space for visualisation after each instruction. If you or another cannot visualise well, that is fine. Instead of trying to visualise or imagine something, allow yourself to feel. Notice any emotions, feelings, or sensations in response to the descriptions below. You might feel peace, relaxation, or a release of emotion. Just be with your experience and know that it is valuable.

Find a peaceful place where you won't be disturbed.

Perceive that you are standing at the edge of a vast ocean with the water lapping at your feet on the shoreline.

Gaze at the horizon, as a stunning sunrise or sunset takes place, whatever feels right for you.

Out of the sun emerges beautiful Mother Mary in flowing robes of gold.

She pours golden light from the sun behind her through her heart and hands and into the top of your head. It flows through you in tingling waves.

The golden light comes out of your feet and continues, flowing into the ocean and filling it with golden light. It flows out of your heart along your arms and out through your palms, filling the space around you.

Rest and receive this for as long as you wish.

Repeat this healing prayer aloud (or quietly in your mind if need be). Imagine that you are sending the words, with love from your heart, to the Divine Mother before you now.

> *I call upon karmic healing and spiritual grace through Mother Mary, who loves me unconditionally. I ask for and accept your divine protection and miraculous grace in all areas of my life, now. I gratefully receive this blessing and the harvest of spiritual grace, which will serve my highest good now. Through divine love and my own free will, may all beings be happy and free.*

Rest for as long as feels right for you.

Sense the golden energy continuing to flow, expanding beyond you, reaching through all dimensions and places to help nourish and soothe all beings in need with the Divine Feminine blessings of grace.

When you are ready to complete the exercise, place your hands on your heart and become aware of your breath. Be aware of the air on your skin and whatever else will help you to ground. It is recommended that you drink some clean water to support the body in integrating your process.

You have completed your sacred practice. Repeat as often as needed to strengthen your relationship with the Divine Mother.

Your purpose is to become what you are — that is why no one can steal your purpose or live your life for you. Each of us needs to find our way home to our heart and to liberate our passion, to live our unique path to the fullest.

As the light within us grows, we cannot help but search for that which inspires us and brings meaning and connection to our lives.

The awakened heart needs to help others thrive. It yearns to create a world filled with hope, consciousness, and compassion. Once you have connected with the passion of your awakened heart, living that calling becomes as natural, essential, and unquestionable as breathing.

Beloved, you don't need to control life. But, you can choose whether you dance with life responsively or resist its flow and feel pushed around by it. How you respond to your circumstances is your choice to make and can be a source of great inner power.

Mother Mary teaches us that the miraculous is meant to happen every day.
It already does! If only we had the eyes of a heart open enough to see it,
we would be sent into states of rapture, gratitude, and wonder, trusting
and curious for whatever unfolds next.

We can be fearful of not being in control of life, of not knowing how it is going to work itself out, or we can be in awe and trust. Choose to surrender into the flow of the Mother's grace, realising that she is within our hearts, never dismissive or forgetful or neglectful.

the
Sacred
Attachment

Shiloh
2004

It is difficult to help someone who won't help themselves.
We have to receive as well as give.

We need courage to make a commitment without trying to control circumstances. We need wisdom to accept the help offered by the Divine Mother and to trust that we are enough, that within us we have what is necessary to keep going and that we know how best to find our way.

It is time to rely on your spiritual principles completely, as a way to live and move in the world. Not only is it safe to do this, but it is the only way to allow the Divine Mother's miraculous love to manifest through you for your benefit and the benefit of all beings.

_____

_____

_____

_____

_____

_____

_____

_____

_____

_____

_____

_____

_____

_____

_____

_____

_____

_____

_____

_____

_____

_____

_____

_____

_____

Change is coming to you now, my dear child. It is a change that has been triggered by the loving prayers held deep within your heart. This change does not have to be difficult for you. Trust in me, and I shall ensure you are supported and shall benefit from all that is unfolding.

Whether you are experiencing change in your life or believe it needs to happen,
pray to her and trust.

*Judgement only hurts when we believe someone has the right to judge us,
rather than realising it is not truth but an expression of a wound in the
person who is judging.*

When another judges us, it is because they cannot love themselves unconditionally, so they are unable to love anyone else in that way. We can hold a place of acceptance for them, and what they are learning, without being brought down by their wounding.

Vulnerability can be powerful when accompanied by an open,
self-loving, and divinely trusting heart.

Our Lady of Radiant Grace
hears the prayers
of the world
and
the ones hidden
in my heart
She
is merciful and
understanding
and
she calls
me one
of Her own

A prayer for healing all hearts: "Beloved Mother, restore my faith in myself and my realisation of my innate purity. May my self-love help others realise their eternal innocence, so that all humanity may act from truth rather than misplaced shame and guilt. May our hearts be free and blessed by your love."

The Divine Feminine holds a space for love, acceptance, truth, and compassion so that sacred, conscious masculinity can emerge in the human heart. Healed masculine consciousness allows us to say yes or no based on our heart's values, which are not blindly adopted from our family or society but distilled from our innermost feelings and soul wisdom.

Even when we are struggling, we can choose to focus on the light within and stay present. Sometimes the struggle is in completely letting go, and facing the final resistance, before being done with a pattern or a habit — when we are on the cusp of true freedom to choose to live, relate, and be in a more self-loving and self-honouring way.

Open your heart to unconditional love and know that you are spiritually protected and supported in all aspects of your life. Remember to ask for help daily. You can do so now by saying: "Mother Mary, please bless and assist me in all ways for the spiritual benefit of all beings."

There are plenty of times when we have to grow into our heartfelt vision.
Sometimes, however, the vision has to grow in order to be worthy of us!
There is something more worthy meant for you. Open your heart and mind
to the possibility of increasing grace in your life.

Sometimes we may hide the truth of what we feel, even from ourselves,
because we are scared of what may come as a result of being honest. Yet
truth, when expressed sincerely from the heart, allows healing to take place.

It is only in letting go that we are able to open up and receive.

She gives
Birth
to
Living Waters

the gratitude journey is a path of cultivating presence

Your time of darkness is swiftly drawing to a close, and soon you shall welcome a new day, a new era, and a new blessing.

The Divine Mother is with us always, even when we are confronted with the very thing we wanted to avoid the most. A letting go that requires greater trust than we have ever had to summon is now being asked of us. Within her care, we will grow through the transition into the larger life awaiting us.

It is your trust that paves the way to the inner gate, opening it wide and allowing you to discover the divine treasures within your heart and soul.

*Signs of spiritual growth are subtle at first and yet, eventually, evidence of
our inner work becomes so obvious that our world is transformed. Before the
transformation bears fruit, we must labour with great trust and without any signs
of success on the horizon. This takes courage and wisdom.*

It takes a brave soul to rely on the feelings of the heart to guide the way, rather than depending on logic, the opinions of others, or expectations of how things 'should' be done. Your heart possesses such courage.

Do not be afraid to trust the quiet voice within that may tell you to wait where others say jump or may ask you to dive in where others say it cannot be done.

The love that flows through a being that is sure of divine protection is
a powerful force capable of liberating hearts and dismantling negative
power structures.

_____

_____

_____

_____

_____

_____

_____

_____

_____

_____

_____

_____

_____

_____

_____

_____

_____

_____

_____

_____

_____

_____

_____

_____

An empowering prayer for all: "Our Lady who Prevents Interference, Mother Mary, who loves me unconditionally, I call upon your healing grace, divine protection, love, and assistance, now. Be with me now. Block all obstruction on my path of love. My heart and focus dwell upon you, bathed in your holy grace. May all beings be happy and free."

Torn open by suffering, your heart has become vulnerable and compassionate.
Strengthened through joy, your soul has become infused with the light of spirit and
accepting of all of life. You are exquisite.